The RHINE HOUSE
BERINGER VINEYARDS

The
RHINE HOUSE
— ❖ —
BERINGER VINEYARDS
Napa Valley's Historic Estate

Photographed by CHARLES O'REAR

Written by DAPHNE LARKIN

CONTENTS

*Previous pages: At dusk, lights of the Rhine House illuminate a magnificent view
of the Victorian building (left). The vines of Chabot Vineyard grace a peaceful landscape among rolling hills
during the summer growing season near St. Helena (right).
Opposite: Visitors entering Beringer Vineyards' historic Rhine House
in Napa Valley see two large stained glass windows with the letter "B" on either side of the Foyer's grand staircase.
These three-foot windows are among 41 stained glass panels that were commissioned by Frederick Beringer
during the mansion's construction in 1883 and 1884.*

MOUNTAIN VINEYA[RD]
OF
BERINGER BROTHERS

(LEMME 280 ACRES)

SAINT HELENA VILLAGE, NAPA Co.

STATE OF CALIFORNIA

1886

5 CHAINS to 1 MILE
SCALE: 16 INCHES to 1 MILE
1:39585 of NATURE

SOUTH EAST OF S.W. QUARTER OF SECTION 26.

SOUTH WEST OF S.E. QUARTER OF SECTION

NORTH EAST OF N.E. QUARTER OF SEC. 34.

NORTH WEST OF N.W. QUARTER OF SEC. 35.

PATCH		No.			TOTAL
PATCH	A,	No. I.	GOLDEN CHASSELAS	1,400 VINES	
"	"	II.	CARIGNAN	1,533 "	
"	"	III.	MATARO	720 "	TOTAL, 4,181 VIN[ES]
"	"	IV.	CANTAL	528 "	
"	B,	I.	BLACK PINOT	866 "	
"	"	II.	CANTAL	2,390 "	
"	"	III.	SAUVIGNON	2,280 "	5,736
"	"	IV.	LENOIRE	200 "	
"	"	V.	ORCHARD		
"	C,	I.	CHASSELAS FOUNT	2,947 "	3,535
"	"	I.	GOLD. CHASSELAS	588 "	
"	D,	I.	ZINFANDEL	456 "	3,218
"	"	II.	GOLD. CHASSELAS	831 "	
"	"	III.		1,931 "	
"	E,	I.	CARIGNAN	3,127 "	
"	"	II.	GRENACH	1,886 "	
"	"	III.	ZINFANDEL	642 "	
"	"	IV.	CARIGNAN	987 "	
"	"	V.	BURGER	2,632 "	
"	"	VI.	CABERNET	1,081 "	20,917
"	"	VII.	MATARO	2,429 "	
"	"	VIII.	CANTAL	1,683 "	
"	"	IX.	CARIGNAN	3,226 "	
"	"	X.	CABERNET	1,045 "	
"	"	XI.	SAUVIGNON	429 "	
"	"	XII.	RIESLING	1,800 "	
"	F,	I.	ZINFANDEL	1,600 "	
"	"	II. & III.	CHARBONO	4,610 "	16,319
"	"	IV.	ZINFANDEL	6,361 "	
"	"		BURGER	3,748 "	
"	G,	I.	BURGER	3,704 "	
"	"	II.	RIESLING	1,232 "	5,214
"	"	III.	ZINFANDEL (Section 35)	194 "	
"	"	IV.	BURGUNDY	84 "	
"	H,	I.	ZINFANDEL	3,393 "	
"	"	II.	SAUVIGNON	3,071 "	
"	"	III.	RIESLING	2,424 "	11,502
"	"	IV.	CANTAL	1,694 "	
"	"	V.	CARIGNAN	920 "	
			TOTAL	70,622 VIN[ES]	

Chapter One

HERITAGE

BERINGER

FOUNDING BERINGER VINEYARDS

Jacob Beringer left his home in Germany to start a new life in America in 1868. His older brother, Frederick, had settled happily in New York five years earlier, but city life did not appeal to Jacob. Having worked in cellars in his home country and been intrigued by tales of a mild climate and ideal land for growing grapes in California, Jacob traveled by train in 1869 to San Francisco and then on to Napa Valley. There he went to work as cellar foreman for Charles Krug, one of the first commercial wineries in the area. In 1875, when 215 acres in St. Helena came up for sale, he convinced Frederick to be the primary financier of the property and the two brothers founded Beringer Brothers Winery, now Beringer Vineyards. With Napa Valley's warm days and cool nights, a wide variety of soils, and surrounding mountain ranges protecting the valley from temperature extremes, Jacob and Frederick knew it was a place where grapes could thrive. It was the beginning of a journey that would forever change the landscape of Napa Valley and would establish Beringer Vineyards as a winery with one of the longest histories in America.

Previous pages: An 1886 map defines Beringer Brothers' mountain vineyards north of St. Helena (left).
Bottles stored in Beringer's underground caves in the 1930s still reside in the old winery's caves (right).
Opposite: Brothers Jacob (left), and Frederick Beringer (right), pose before a wooden wine cask in their winery caves in 1885.
Redwood was introduced as the wood of choice for barrel aging and storing wine during the early
years of the wine industry in northern California. The native wood was readily available, resistant to insects and
produced large sections of boards sufficient to construct big tanks. During this period, winemakers
in Napa Valley also used oak barrels imported from Europe.

OLD STONE WINERY & CAVES

The Old Stone Winery was one of the first buildings constructed, and the brothers carefully chose its location against a hillside. They made a road in the hill behind the winery so wagons could unload grapes into the crusher on the third floor allowing juice to flow by

gravity into the fermenting tanks on the second floor. The wine would then flow down to the ground floor for aging in casks before being bottled. About the same time the winery was being constructed, laborers began hand-chiseling 1,000 linear feet of rock tunnels in the hill behind the winery. Taking several years to complete, the labyrinth of tunnels provided a constant temperature of 58 degrees Fahrenheit, the perfect temperature for aging and storing wine. Today Beringer Vineyards still ages wine in the caves of the Old Stone Winery.

THE RHINE HOUSE & HUDSON HOUSE

In 1883, Frederick Beringer began construction of his new 17-room mansion—the Rhine House—based on the design of his ancestral home in Germany. Frederick wanted the Rhine House to have prominent placement on the site, and soon determined the location should be where his brother Jacob's home, now the Hudson House, stood.

Above: Built in 1877, Beringer's Old Stone Winery today houses retail sales and is the portal to the winery's caves. In 2001, the Beringer estate was recognized as an Historic District by the National Register of Historic Places.
Opposite above: Frederick Beringer (center) stands with brother Jacob (left) and Jacob's son Charles in front of the cellar with workers in 1895.
Opposite below: Master winemaker Jacob Beringer in his cellar.

The Hudson House was moved 200 feet north, rolled on logs, to accommodate Frederick's monument to his success in Napa Valley. Today, the Hudson House serves as Beringer Vineyards' Culinary Arts Center and the Rhine House is the center of Beringer's reserve and library tastings. Here, in the crown jewel of the Beringer estate, guests can enjoy a taste of wine while relaxing in Frederick's library or on his porch overlooking the expansive lawns and lush gardens.

Opposite: Fall colors descend on Marston Vineyard in the Spring Mountain District west of St. Helena. Marston is one of many prized and sustainably farmed vineyards throughout Napa Valley that provide top quality grapes for Beringer wines while keeping with the winery's commitment to the environment. Above: Nineteenth century portraits of Beringer Brothers co-founders, Frederick (left), and Jacob Beringer (right).

Opposite and above: Elm trees planted by the Beringer brothers
in front of their winery provided shade for Jacob Beringer and his daughter
Bertha who pose with workers in 1886 on the wagon trail
north of St. Helena. Today, that same wagon trail directs visitors on
State Highway 29 through St. Helena's beloved "Tunnel of Elms,"
a famous landmark in Napa Valley.

OVER THE YEARS

Beringer Vineyards has hosted generations of guests and has consistently garnered awards and accolades for its quality portfolio of wines. This legacy of fine wines and hospitality has been celebrated since the Rhine House opened its doors in 1884 and the Beringer family began welcoming guests to a constant stream of dinner parties, teas and other events. After Prohibition ended, Beringer became the first winery in Napa Valley to offer public tours, launching the area's wine tourism business in 1934. Tourists went on guided tours through the underground caves, the Old Stone Winery and the vineyards before purchasing wine. Soon Beringer was a top destination for visitors from San Francisco and Los Angeles. In 1967, Beringer Vineyards was named a State Historical Landmark.

TODAY

The legacy of Beringer Vineyards that Frederick and Jacob Beringer created so many years ago lives on. It is a legacy of creating memorable wines from great Napa Valley vineyards as much as a legacy of offering warm hospitality and welcome to all. In 1972, the Rhine House was placed on the National Register for Historic Places and, in 2001, the Beringer estate was placed on the list as well. Beringer Vineyards holds the distinction of being the oldest continuously operating winery in Napa Valley.

Beringer family members and employees celebrate the end of Prohibition with jugs, bottles and barrels of wine in front of the Old Stone Winery. Beringer Brothers Winery continued to operate during Prohibition by providing sacramental wines to churches and selling dried grapes to home winemakers.

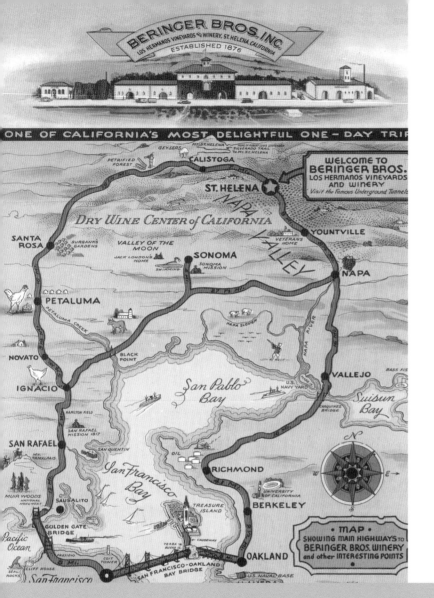

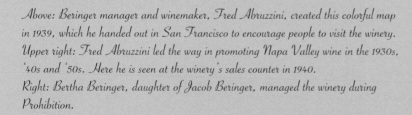

Above: Beringer manager and winemaker, Fred Abruzzini, created this colorful map in 1939, which he handed out in San Francisco to encourage people to visit the winery.
Upper right: Fred Abruzzini led the way in promoting Napa Valley wine in the 1930s, '40s and '50s. Here he is seen at the winery's sales counter in 1940.
Right: Bertha Beringer, daughter of Jacob Beringer, managed the winery during Prohibition.

Above: Jacob Beringer entertains winery guests in 1904, establishing the legacy of hospitality that has become a Beringer tradition.
Upper right: Arched doorways in the Old Stone Winery form the backdrop for Jacob's daughters, Bertha (top right) and Martha (top center), with friends.
Right: An original stained glass window still decorates the Old Stone Winery today.

SPARKLER BRAND

NET CONTENTS
4/5 QUART

ALCOHOL
12 % BY VOLUME

MONOGRAM
BERINGER BROS., INC.

SPARKLER
BRAND
TRADE MARK   REGISTERED
CALIFORNIA MOSELLE
CARBONATED
PRODUCED AND BOTTLED BY
BERINGER BROS., INC.
ST. HELENA, CALIF.
BONDED WINERY NO. 46 - 1

Opposite: Beringer employees, including Ramona Gooden (right), the soon-to-be bride of Otto Beringer, Jr., show off a promotional bottle of Sparkler wine in 1935. Left: Colorful labels bring attention to wines, including this undated label for Sparkler, an effervescent wine that may have been a California version of the German sparkling Sekt. Below: Visitors line up for Beringer's first winery tour in 1934, marking Napa Valley's entry into the hospitality business following the end of Prohibition. More than 5,000 people accepted the invitation of Fred Abruzzini (center, in white jacket) to tour the winery that day, and by 1940 more than 25,000 were visiting Beringer annually. Over the years, some five million visitors have been guests of Beringer Vineyards.

CHRONOLOGY OF BERINGER VINEYARDS

1869　Jacob Beringer arrives in the Napa Valley and becomes cellar foreman for Charles Krug, one of the first commercial winemakers in Napa Valley.

1875　Frederick and Jacob purchase what will become the heart of the Beringer Vineyards estate—215 acres in St. Helena. The $14,500 purchase price includes the Hudson House where Jacob makes his home.

1876　Jacob and Frederick Beringer establish Beringer Brothers Winery and oversee their first harvest. Jacob is the winery's first winemaker, and Frederick is the financier.

1877　The Old Stone Winery and cellar are completed and laborers begin hand-chiseling 1,000 linear feet of rock tunnels for aging and storing wine.

1883　Frederick Beringer begins building his 17-room mansion—the Rhine House—on the former site of the Hudson House, which is moved 200 feet north. The Rhine House is completed in 1884.

1887　Beringer wines win awards at the Mechanic's Institute Exposition in San Francisco, the first of many they will receive over the years.

1901　Frederick Beringer passes away, his widow moves to San Francisco and Jacob Beringer takes over the winery.

1915　Jacob Beringer passes away. The following year, two of Jacob's children, Charles and Bertha Beringer, take the winery reins.

1918　Prohibition is enacted but Beringer is one of two wineries in Napa to remain open by selling sacramental wine to the Church. Bertha Beringer manages the winery throughout Prohibition, which is repealed in 1933.

1934　Beringer becomes the first winery in Napa Valley to offer public tours, launching the area's tourist wine business.

1972　The Rhine House is listed on the National Register of Historic Places.

1977　The 1977 Private Reserve Cabernet Sauvignon marks the first vintage of the Private Reserve program at Beringer Vineyards, and subsequent vintages continue to garner top awards and critical acclaim.

1990　Beringer 1986 Cabernet Sauvignon is named No. 1 Wine of the Year by Wine Spectator.

1996　Beringer 1994 Chardonnay is named No. 1 Wine of the Year by Wine Spectator—the first time a white wine won the award. Beringer is the first and only winery to have both a white and a red wine named No. 1 Wine of the Year.

2001　Beringer Vineyards celebrates its 125th anniversary and the distinction of being the oldest continuously operating winery in Napa Valley. The Beringer estate is placed on the National Register of Historic Places.

The stained glass windows in the Rhine House, some of which are signed by the artists, are considered
rare and valuable and were conserved to their original beauty and brilliance during the restoration. This 18-inch window
provides a brilliant display of color in a room tucked behind the master bedroom on the second floor.

Chapter Two

THE RHINE HOUSE

BUILDING THE RHINE HOUSE

When Frederick Beringer began construction of the Rhine House in 1883, he set out to build an elegant mansion that would reflect his family's impressive old German home at Mainz-on-Rhine. As the primary financier of Beringer Brothers Winery, Frederick picked

the best site on the property for his home, an oaky knoll where his brother's house stood overlooking the property's sweeping grounds and the country road beyond. His brother Jacob agreed to move his 1850 farmhouse, now the Hudson House, two hundred feet north to accommodate his older brother's request. Frederick hired the German architect Albert Schroepfer of San Francisco to oversee the design of his 17-room mansion, and began building the Rhine House.

With 17 rooms built at a cost of $28,000, the building was an extravagant display at the time. Its construction was catalogued along the way by society and local media, and upon completion was reported in the local newspaper to be "the nicest house in town" and the pride of St. Helena. In 1883, there was a celebration as the cornerstone was laid for the Rhine House. The majestic building was listed with the National Register of Historic Places and designated a Napa Valley landmark in 1972.

Previous page: With renovation completed in 2008, the Rhine House today appears with lush landscaping, new walkways and an improved infrastructure, including geothermal heating and cooling and earthquake retrofitting. The limestone, brick and redwood Victorian building with its gables, dormer windows, porches and steeples is a unique treasure among Napa Valley's many other wineries. Above: The hand of an artist touches up a hand of the Shakespearean knight on the front entry door of the Rhine House during renovation in 2008. Opposite: A fountain decorated with a grape motif greets visitors entering the Rhine House.

Above: A 360-degree panoramic view of the Rhine House Foyer highlights exquisite design details throughout the building—rich wall colors, redwood ceilings, mahogany wood carvings, inlaid floors, hand-stenciled patterns and the extensive, decorative use of stained glass.
Left: Doorknobs, hinges, lamps, and fireplace décor accent rooms on the first floor.

THE RESTORATION

To preserve the rich tradition and legacy of the Rhine House and Beringer Vineyards, a full-scale restoration of the Rhine House was undertaken in 2007, along with several other buildings on the grounds. With the lofty goal of returning the Rhine House to its original splendor, a team of gifted artisans and master craftsmen began restoring the house while maintaining its historical integrity.

During the two-year restoration, hidden treasures were uncovered throughout the mansion. One such discovery provided a glimpse into an earlier time when—as today—the Rhine House served as the heart of the developing Napa Valley lifestyle and social gatherings. Underneath wallpaper in the Foyer, the artisans found a hand-stenciled pattern bordering the ceiling with a German message of welcome to visitors entering the magnificent home.

Opposite: Artists for Nzilani Glass Conservation guide a stained glass panel for the front entry door back into place during the summer of 2008. Many of the 41 stained glass windows were removed before being conserved. Conservation methods stabilize what remains and stops degradation while retaining the quality of the piece as it was originally created.
Above: The letter "T" serves as the centerpiece for this six-foot glass panel over the entry doors. The "T" replaced Frederick Beringer's logo after Charles and Mary Teague bought the Rhine House in 1914 from Frederick's widow. Later the Beringer family would once again own the house and property.

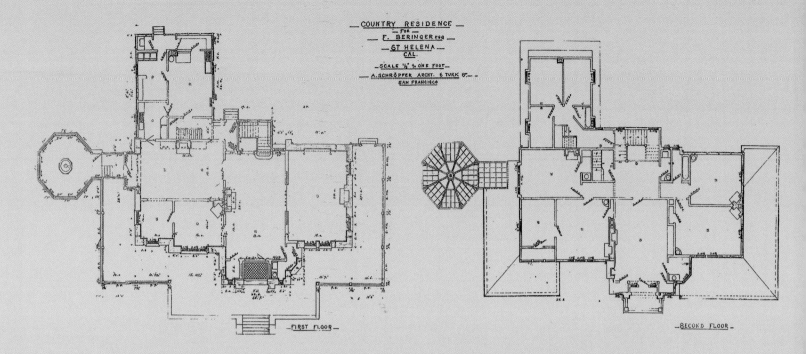

COUNTRY RESIDENCE
FOR
F. BERINGER ESQ
ST HELENA
CAL.
SCALE ⅛" to ONE FOOT
A. SCHRÖPFER ARCHT. 6 TURK ST.
SAN FRANCISCO

FIRST FLOOR

SECOND FLOOR

As layer after layer of the mansion's rooms were peeled back during the restoration, Frederick's grand vision for the Rhine House became resoundingly clear: it is a stunning icon of Victorian architecture and art. With 41 glittering stained glass panels reflecting colored light throughout the house, stenciled paint work on the walls, hand-carved wood panels and cabinets, inlaid floors of imported woods, embossed ornamental wallpaper, and redwood, oak, mahogany and cherry paneling, the building displays many artistic touches that reveal Frederick's eye for detail and design in his creation of the masterpiece that is the Rhine House today.

Above: Original floor plans for the Rhine House included a glass-enclosed conservatory on the south side, which was built but later destroyed by earthquake. The floor design remains the same today.
Opposite: As one of three windows in the Music Room, now the Ed Sbragia Room on the second floor, this window depicts a French horn. Sbragia was the sixth winemaker in the winery's history.

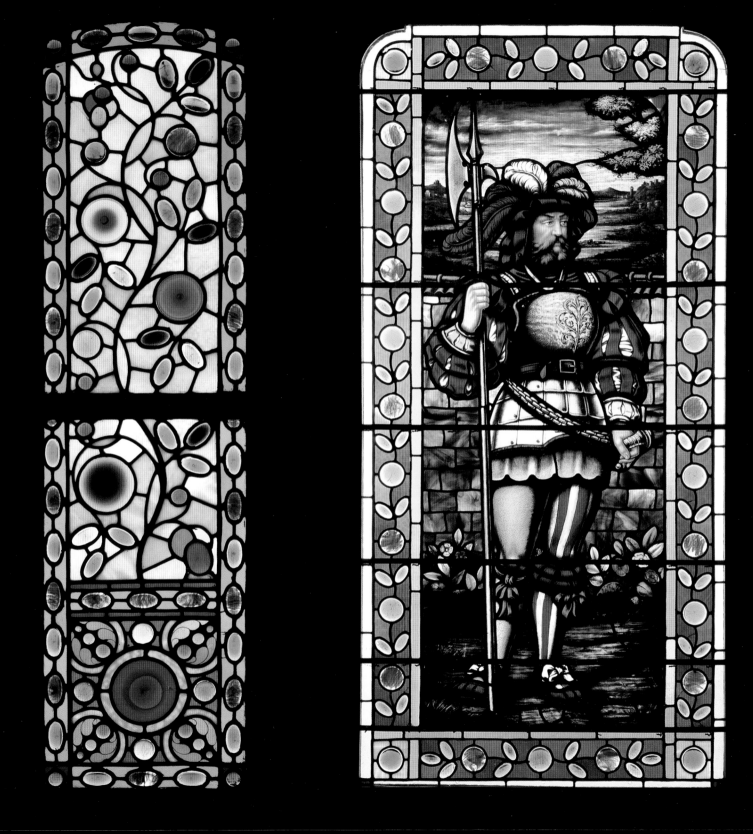

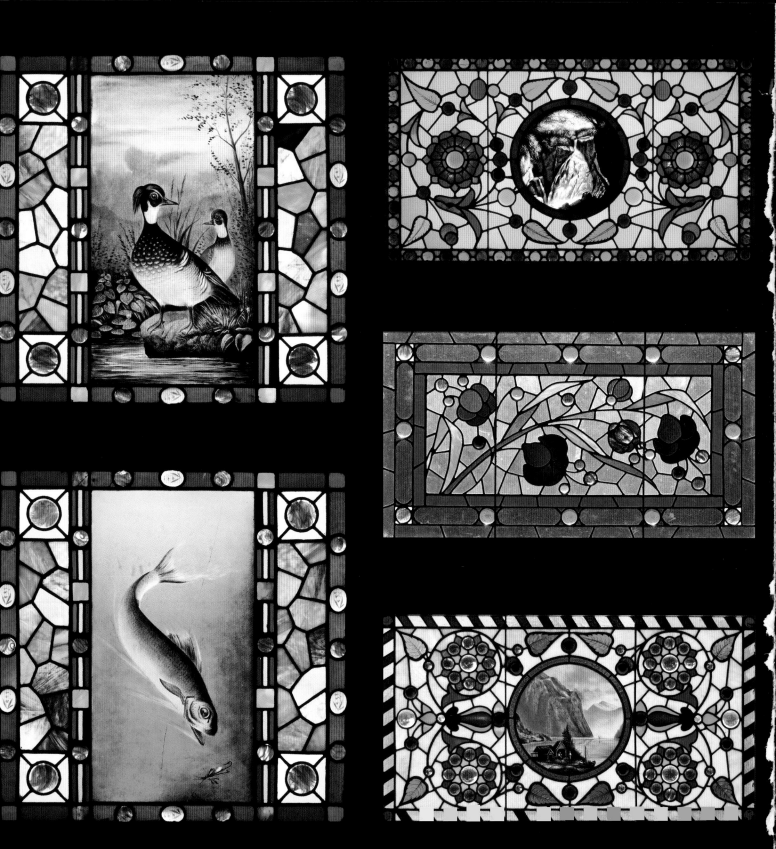

STAINED GLASS: *Frederick Beringer commissioned artists to create 41 stained glass windows for the Rhine House in the 1880s, reflecting his wealth, good taste and appreciation of art and architecture. In an era when mansions had one or two stained glass windows at most, the large collection of Victorian* *decorative glass in the Rhine House was rare. The ornate panels are a combination of stained, painted, enameled and leaded glass, each featuring hand-painted jeweled borders and exquisite roundels that tie them together throughout the house. Scenes of butterflies and wildflowers, game and trout,*

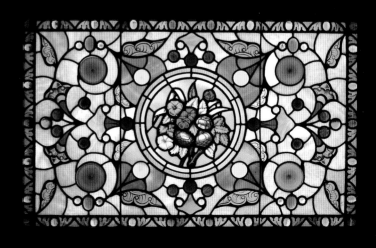

and still life designs are seen along with those of the American West. The origin of stained glass windows is obscure, but the art form as we know it today arose with the beginning of substantial church building and was first documented in German and French churches in the 10th century. During the early 19th century, the art of stained glass window making was revived in churches in England and by the end of the century stained glass windows had become popular in the homes of wealthy Americans.

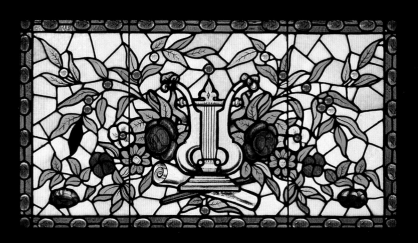

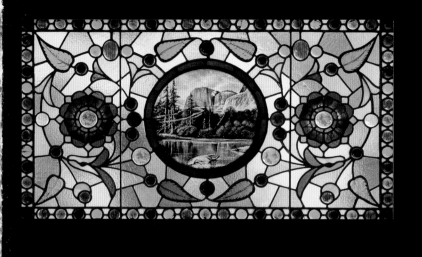

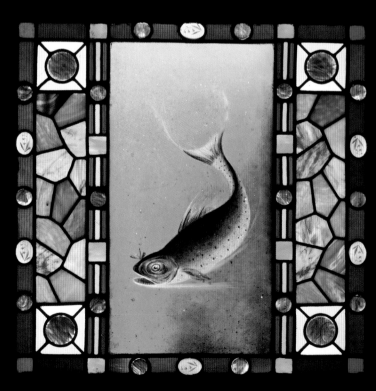

STAINED GLASS WINDOWS

Perhaps the most dazzling feature of the Rhine House is its 41 original stained glass and leaded panels—rare in an era when grand homes had one or two such windows at most. Created for Frederick Beringer by various artists, the panels of decorative Belgian art nouveau-style glass cost $6,000—nearly a quarter of total construction costs of the Rhine House. While the windows have different design themes relating to each room—fish, fowl, fruit, and wine in the Dining Room and butterflies and flowers in the Parlor Room, for example—the glass panels share overarching components popular during the Victorian era. Throughout, hand painted jeweled borders and roundels tie the windows together to create a stunning display of color and light from every angle in the house.

Previous pages: Shakespearean knights greet guests as they enter
Beringer's Rhine House through the majestic double front doors. Long believed to represent the faces
of Frederick and Jacob Beringer, the doors illuminate the grand Foyer.
Opposite and above: The original Library today offers visitors a selection of books about wine and
wine growing countries. In this evening photo, William Shakespeare keeps
watch from the window while symbols of a globe and theater mask appear on either side.

Above: A frog, a shell and plants in this stained glass window suggest a scene of a pond.
Left: A stained glass ceiling lamp lights a second floor room of the Rhine House.
Opposite: Conservationist Ariana Makau of Nzilani Glass Conservation uses her specialized expertise to place a final touch on an outdoor scene in the Laurie Hook Room, formerly Frederick Jr.'s bedroom, on the second floor. Laurie Hook is only the seventh winemaker in the winery's history since Beringer opened its doors in 1876.

Two of the most delicate stained glass windows in the Rhine House grace the downstairs Parlor Room where visitors taste fine Beringer wines. The theme of flowers, butterflies, and dragonflies adds a look different from any of the other windows and offers a vision into the variety Frederick Beringer wanted visitors to experience when he constructed the Rhine House.

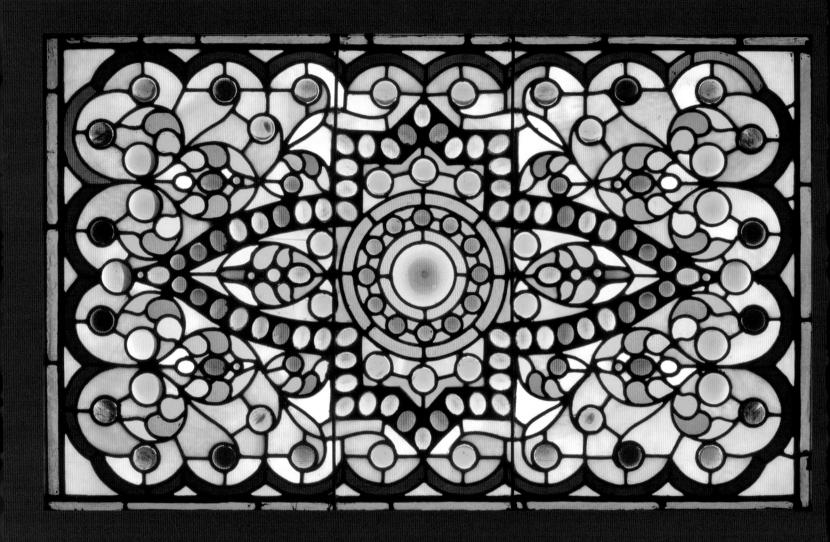

Opposite: The corner Drawing Room on the first floor displays unique patterns glittering with multiple colors of stained glass.
Above: This fruit still life made an appetizing addition to the rich décor in the Dining Room.

Hunting scenes, common in the Beringer family's homeland of Germany,
dominate the stained glass windows in the grand staircase leading to the second floor.

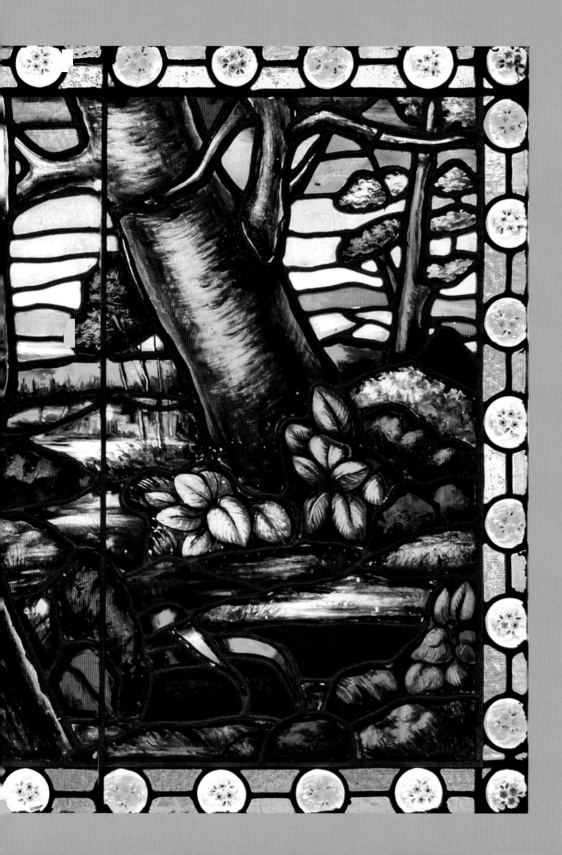

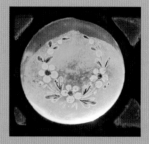

Left: A three-foot-wide stained glass window depicting a forest scene looks down over the Owl Room, originally the nursery.
Above: Bordering several windows are circles of glass, only two inches in size.
Each of these is painted with miniature flowers.

WOODWORK

Old world craftsmanship at its best can be seen in the woodwork throughout the Rhine House. The lavish use of different varieties of wood in the interior, much of it bearing detailed hand-carved patterns, was considered unusual and innovative in the late 1800s. Every room yields visually interesting and complex layers of carved wood. During restoration, artisans replaced portions of the mahogany-stained cherry paneling and stripped away a century's worth of varnish and wax from the hardwood floors before repairing and refinishing them.

Opposite: The intimate corner of the first floor Drawing Room is popular for private wine tastings.
Above: Wood panels surround the Dining Room while ornate hand-carved cabinets line the wall on either side of
the fireplace, reflecting the earthy Victorian color tones popular in the day. The Dining Room, with its stained glass scenes of fish
and fowl, was a gracious setting for the Beringers' large dinner parties. Today, the room invites visitors to peruse wines and gifts.

Opposite: Napa woodcarver Steve Booth prepares templates to create wall carvings on the interior of the Rhine House. To create the acorn-and-leaf theme carvings, Booth used specialized techniques similar to the original ones employed when the building was constructed in 1883.

Above left: Inlaid wood panels of redwood, oak and cherry line the perimeter of the floors in every main room in the house. Woods for the inlaid pattern, some of which were imported, have been restored to their original look.

Above right: A staircase railing of carved oak rises toward the second floor.

Willkommen

wer mit Herz

und Hand

Sich je in

Freundschaft

begegnet

FRESCOS

When layers of old wallpaper dating back 124 years were removed from the walls of the Rhine House in the Foyer and the Parlor Room, the original plaster walls were uncovered for the first time in many years. Further investigation revealed a hidden treasure: evidence of hand-stenciled patterns with a fresco of a repeating teardrop motif. The focal point of the frescos were banners that ran along the top of the room containing a message written in German: "Welcome, who with heart and hand will ever in friendship meet." In total, a palette of over 20 colors was used in the patterns created for these two rooms with a focus on pink, blue and green, repeating the colors of the surrounding stained glass windows.

The restoration team conserved the frescos with specialized techniques that protect them from degradation going forward. A team of artists covered the original frescos with a protective sealant and applied a new coat of paint over them so that the paintwork displays all the vibrancy and richness it once had over 100 years ago.

This hand-stenciled message of welcome was discovered beneath layers of wallpaper in the grand entry to the Rhine House during restoration. Today, as over 100 years ago, visitors are greeted with: "Welcome, who with heart and hand will ever in friendship meet."

STRUCTURAL INNOVATIONS

Keeping in the tradition of innovation that Frederick Beringer set in place so long ago, while echoing the winery's commitment to the community and the environment, the restoration included installing a geothermal heating and cooling system. Digging three hundred feet into a geothermal field in the front lawn of the Rhine House, experts designed a GeoExchange system where water is forced through a system of underground pipes that maintain a consistent temperature of 55 to 65 degrees Fahrenheit. Circulated through the house, the water heats and cools while conserving energy and creating a more sustainable structure for the future.

The Rhine House also received seismic strengthening during restoration to prevent damage from tremors or earthquakes. The core of the house was strengthened with steel to ensure that it will remain sound for generations to come.

THE BERINGER LEGACY

Restoring the Rhine House to its original grandeur celebrates the foundation on which the Beringer brothers built this legendary estate and winery. Today, visitors flock to Beringer by the thousands each year to tour the Rhine House and its beautiful grounds, taste superb wines and experience the warmth of Napa Valley hospitality. The rich history of the Rhine House and the winery's estate are parallel to Beringer Vineyards' unique legacy of excellence in hospitality, vineyards and winemaking since 1876.

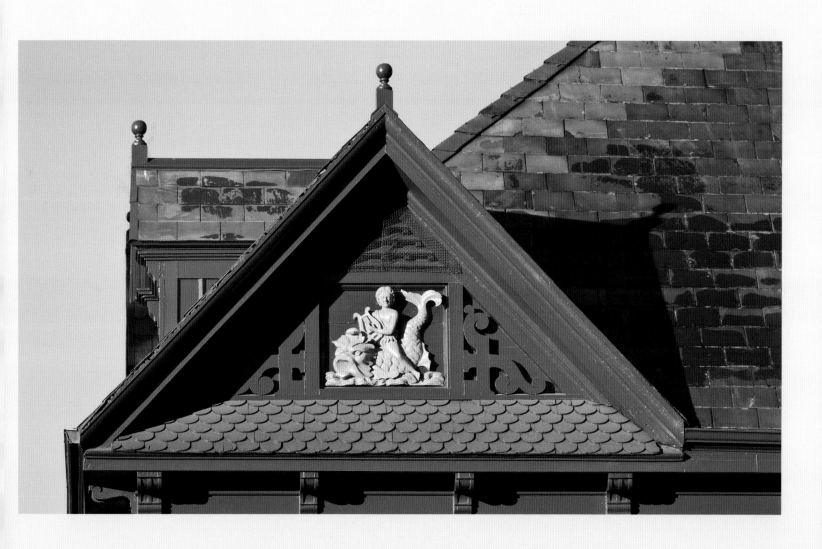

A symbol of the Arion Society, which Frederick Beringer was affiliated with in New York and which
introduced German music appreciation to America, adorns a third floor dormer on the front of the Rhine House.
The woodcarving is one of many design details he commissioned for his new home.

Chapter Three

A LEGACY OF WINEMAKING

VINEYARDS

Since Beringer Brothers Winery opened its doors in 1876, it has been dedicated to making memorable wines from great Napa Valley vineyards. Outstanding wines begin on the vine, and winemakers and viticulturists work hand in hand to ensure that the optimal growing conditions result in the highest quality fruit at each vineyard. Beringer's long history in the Napa Valley has allowed the winery to establish a remarkable collection of vineyards for its wines, encompassing a variety of appellations, each with distinctive soils, microclimates and terrain. Location, soil, weather and vines can all affect the many flavors and aromas found in wine, and the winemakers strive to create the finest expression of the vineyards with each vintage. Beringer's reserve wines have consistently received great acclaim for their concentration of flavor, aging ability, and their elegant expression of Napa Valley terroir.

Beringer's vineyards extend well beyond the first acres on the original estate that Jacob and Frederick Beringer purchased. Vineyards on Howell Mountain provide Cabernet Sauvignon and Merlot grapes of intensity and depth, while those in Yountville at the valley floor lend lush tropical flavors to the reserve Chardonnay. With over two thousand acres in the Napa Valley that contribute to the reserve tier of Beringer wines, the quality and location of these vineyards are unrivaled.

Previous pages: Caves dug by laborers in the 1870s still age some of Beringer's wines today (left).
This label appears on bottles placed in a corner of the caves in the 1930s (right).
Opposite: Oak trees frame the linear vine rows at Beringer's Knights Valley Vineyard in Sonoma County.
Many of the winery's most popular wines are produced from grapes grown here.
Above: Chardonnay grapes are ready to harvest at Gamble Ranch Vineyard near Oakville.

PRIVATE RESERVE PROGRAM

In 1977, Beringer Vineyards created its Private Reserve Program to make handcrafted, world-class wine from the finest vineyards with each vintage. Consistently thereafter, Beringer Private Reserve wine has been released to great acclaim. Since the winery's estab-

lishment in 1876, there have been only seven winemakers at the helm, each contributing to the respected legacy in winemaking. After more than three decades, Beringer's goal to make the best Cabernet Sauvignon that Napa Valley can produce has been achieved, surpassing even Jacob Beringer's ambitious vision for the winery.

Beringer's legacy in the Napa Valley has blossomed from a rich history, a warm tradition of hospitality, and an unparalleled collection of wines. These wines have been recognized for their excellence by wine lovers, collectors, and critics worldwide, and can be found on top wine lists throughout the world. A singular dedication to quality from vineyard to bottle is what makes these wines, and Beringer Vineyards, so exceptional.

Above: A vineyard manager determines grapes are nearly ready for harvest when the skin breaks easily.
Opposite: Cabernet Sauvignon grapes hang from a unique arbor system at Knights Valley Vineyard. This style
of growing grapes on a trellis represents one of many techniques used to produce the best grapes for wine.

Opposite: Workers harvest Cabernet Sauvignon grapes from Beringer's Home Vineyard in St. Helena. Home Vineyard, which was planted when the Beringer brothers purchased the winery property in 1875, is across York Creek and behind the Rhine House. Today the vineyard produces some of the winery's most prized grapes.

Above left: A sign marks the rootstock found in this row planted in 1989 at Steinhauer Vineyard on Howell Mountain near Angwin.

Above right: Grapes fly through the air from a picker's box before being driven to the winery in one-half ton bins.

Right: A field worker sharpens a picking knife during harvest.

Above: A wine cask hand-carved in Germany in the mid-19th century provides visitors a glimpse into the winery's early days. Opposite: Caves behind the Old Stone Winery provide a trip back into history. Hand dug over a period of several years in the late 1870s, the caves provide a constant temperature of 58 degrees Fahrenheit for wine storing and aging. Here, Fred Abruzzini (background) climbs a ladder to top off wine barrels while a worker repairs a wooden cask in the late 1930s. Today visitors are guided through historic tunnels during tours of Beringer Vineyards.

Opposite above: Bottles of 70-year-old wine rest in a private tasting room in the caves at Beringer.
Opposite below: Until recent years, these oak casks aged hundreds of gallons of wine
and now they are on view for visitors to see in the Old Stone Winery.
Above: The letter "B" welcomes guests to a private tasting room tucked deep inside the winery's caves.

This edition published in 2009 by
Wineviews Publishing LLC
Box 193, St. Helena, California 94574

ISBN-13: 978-0-9625227-7-2
Printed in China

Design: Leslie Barry and Jennifer Barry, Jennifer Barry Design, Fairfax, California
Layout Production: Kristen Hall

View additional photography at: www.wineviews.com